Penmanship Poets

Mahogany L. Browne

Destroy, Rebuild & Other Reconstructions of the Human Muscle

Sean Patrick Conlon

The Pornography Diaries

Eboni

Grits

Falu

10 Things I Want To Say To A Black Man

Dasha Kelly

Hershey Eats Peanuts

Jive Poetic

Typeface: Poems & A Bunch of Other What-Not

Jaha Zainabu

The Corners of My Shaping

Lauren Zuniga

The Nickel Tour

www.Penmanshipbooks.com

Melissa + Tremone,

You make friends everyday, but making family is rare. Thank you,

WJ

Published by Penmanship Books

593 Vanderbilt Avenue, #265

Brooklyn, NY 11238

Copyright © 2009 by William Evans

Cover Art by Valerie Thompson of
Leap Graphics

All rights reserved. This book may
not be reproduced in whole or in part
(except in the case of reviews)
without written permission from
author.

Printed in The United States of
America

10 9 8 7 6 5 4 3 2 1

1

In the Event You are Caught Behind Enemy Lines

A collection of Poems by

William Evans

Part A. Two Requests from a prisoner of war; to see tomorrow's sunrise and that you never become the target of your captor's boredom.

- Other Talents
- Curtain
- Tailored
- Ghetto, Mine
- 21 Gun Salute for Jesse Jackson from Huey P Newton
- In the Event You are Caught Behind Enemy Lines and then Tortured
- Quartered
- Farragut, TN (1:30 pm EST)
- Dear Joseph
- For the Fledgling Masochist – or 10 simple ways to get yourself kicked in the junk
- The Folly in Standing Up

Part B. The boat ride home is not nearly crowded enough.

- Grown Up Ladders
- Feathers Like Hammers (for Clyde Stubblefield)
- La Lluvia Trae Su Nombre
- You Revolution, You
- Forest Fire
- Blacksmith
- Beautiful Biology
- To Dine on Man

Part A. Two Requests from a prisoner of war; to see tomorrow's sunrise and that you never become the target of your captor's boredom.

Other Talents (Miseducation of Black Males)

From the time you emerged from the heavy brush
Your knuckles pussed over and whispering prayers
To absent clouds
A fresh kill slung over your shoulder
Heavier than the blood of your yesterday

They saw your worth

Sized you up like the uniforms
Of Best Men
Told you to hand over the kill
For preparation

Besides

Your talents lie elsewhere
Remember the stop gap
In your usefulness boy

The youth of a black male
Is often wasted on deciding what
To do with him

They fed you the biggest portion
Of the feast
Kept you strong
Like the kickback
Of a 19th century rifle
Strung tight
Like a tug of war between
The ego of Goliath's

There is salvation in your pushups
Copper reflection
In your grip
Of a blunt instrument

They will spare you the vegetables
Keep the shrubbery
From ever resting on your tongue

What would you need with brain food anyway?
What could you possibly do
With a problem to solve?

No
That's not where your talent lies

They carved you into a boat
Called your suggestions cute and told you not to worry
About the water

If it rains
You row yourself harder than nightfall
Till you find a shelter
Provided for you
Keep the waves from overturning the orders you were
given
Its not like you're responsible for the clean-up
Just do what these wish granters say

Keep a shovel
In your back pocket
You will lose count
Of the number of times
You bury your ambition

When you tire of jumping
Wrap this courage around your neck
And yell
           How High
Off the deck of a slave ship
These waters
Might be too smart to navigate
Swimming is an art form
You don't own the canvas for

That's not where your talent lies

You were ahead of your time
A heroin addict during prohibition
A slum Lord resident
Lost in the shade of pinstripe suits
You live under store front canopies
So you never have to figure out
How the sun works

You are the Red
Before a Harlem Minister

The Casius with Louisville, KY
Foot speed

Better seen
And not heard from
Better seen big
And fast
And compliant
But not heard from

Muscle you cannot control
Is wasted potential
So they gifted you chess pieces
Made out of liquor stores
Rubbed your nose in gun powder
And got you addicted to misfires
Convinced you of a high
That exists in the sliding track
Of a nine-millimeter
The shell ejects sideways
Like the glances you receive
When you interrupt intelligent men
Talking

You are better suited for
Watching the door

In case someone with your shoulders
Arrives unannounced

Better suited for scaling chain-link
Religions and outrunning racehorses

Here is the rub
Your professor would've warned you of
If the world ever needed students
Of your caliber

You will survive a voyage across a storm
That connects your home
To enslavement

The filtration of
Crack into your drinking water

A fallout
When the Panther Party
No longer saw your neighborhood
As a political stronghold

Premed and Proper infielders

Affirmative Action for malt liquor

A steroid stipend

100 meters of free land
As long as you run straight forward
And do it in World Record Time

A 2nd round knockout
Gold Glove handshakes
That leave swelling in your fingers

You are a survivor
Limped away from mousetraps

Carried a noose around your neck
Up Hamburger Hill

Viet Nam friendly fire
A Tuskegee syringe

A Bayou Boycott

22 Million Crabs
Who believe the opening of the barrel is a myth

Dated outside your race
And let them call you

Wasted potential
Like you were a useful savage
Before you found love
In the ivory throat of a believer

A tornado that checks in
On the futures it destroyed

You will confront this nuclear beast in the woods
Sling the kill over your shoulder
Walk until your feet find
A green they do not deserve

The inhabitants will cower at the danger
You slew
And you'll tell them
Don't bother to stand up

This
Is not where your talent lies

Curtain

The stairs coughed dust under each betrayal of flight. His steps fault line split the plush into Burberry gashes not intended to heal. Each boot below sea level groans white flags into his treads. He reaches the Atlantic floor and pivots like a train derailed. Bloodhounds the basement, combing the wind for a virgin taste in his cheeks. A bottle rocket pin drop he can be proud of. A medusa glare ensnares the small table in the corner, an island seceded from idle hands.

You

have curled your legs under you like swept glass from a mother's day vase, keep your arms under the rickety wooden umbrella as if heaven bore acid in its bosom. You feel the clockwork of the floorboards as he drags himself toward the table. A long necked glass woman in his palm, spewing spuds from her throat as he stammers. Puts her to his lips and spills her words down the front of his torn armor. You feel him pendulum toward you, gathering speed he does not control. He can smell future in your soap, upsets his stomach something terrible. He crosses the equator, wants to open your hemisphere. You smell your mother's insides when he reaches for you. Tighten your Venus fly trap around the screwdriver. His wing has fewer feathers than you remember. He Marilyn Monroe's the table cover. You ready the screwdriver between your fingers like a gear shift, imagine putting his neckline in Neutral.

When Officer Turner arrives, you'll tell him you're a good listener, that good girls know how to follow directions. It was just like Officer Turner told you it would be, swing your arm down like yanking open a curtain. Just like yanking open

A curtain.

Tailored

I.
I'm guessing
The first indication was a nod
A gesture with eyelashes we often overlook
     In each other
But not in our prey
Perhaps when we bypassed
Handshakes for chest to chest hugs
It was symptom of our unwillingness
To extend ourselves
Towards each other
Our legs have grown too sturdy
For seesaws

Hell hath
A gravitational pull
On your feet
The older you become
You don't learn these lessons
Alone
Though you practice them as
     Adversaries
Punishing the earth
Underneath warring elephants

II.
Never has a woman
Death by strangulation her legs
Around me like she does
I sweat out my childhood
Every time
     I enter her
The walls swelter under her moans
I am immune to the names
She gives me
Thankful for the unbiased looks
I swallow like a tranquilizer

I marvel how those basketball courts
Never prepared me
Those shotgun passenger tours we spent
Never taught me to recognize your scent

On someone else

Never took your palm print
For a birthmark on her left thigh
Details are the first to go
When you are drowning

III.
If it's any consolation
I have never felt anything as honest
As your third
And fourth knuckle
Searching for answers in my left eye
I left my regrets
In the fracture of your fist
I did not intend to pull up the flowers
Of your garden
To seduce the star
You hung your future on
She roped us both
          Like cattle
Her smile a storm that crashed our ships
Against the rocks
Together
Starboards and anchors floating
In a mass grave
Where we both find familiar faces
But our own surprise us
Neither of us knowing how to shake hands
Without hugging
Or how to say her name without
Showing our fangs
At each other

Ghetto, Mine

Excuse me miss
I believe
You're stepping on my ghetto

Yes
My ghetto

Every broken sidewalk
And oil leaking car of it

Every corner store
And low expectation is mine

I mean ours
Used to be yours

It is both given and birthright
Both bequeathed and left for dead

Like dreams that have become plump
Raised on lard

We are resolute
We are hood
We are so
Gangsta

We are immune to the smell of our own decay

This is my lamp post
My lookout spot
My sewer reeking of a teenage girl's virginity

Don't you cry for her
She was born here

If she's scared now, she'll be a long time dying

But her son
Was born here too

One day
His children gonna bury pops up on 17th Ave
If they ever get to know the bastard

Shit
Like they would ever know themselves
If stop signs didn't fall from the sky

Like the concrete didn't grow tall from Hell
Raised on Satan's tears

But where were you money?

Where were you when I carved complacency
On the back of my eyeballs?

Where were you when I wore a sag in my jeans
Because mom used my belt to tie off her forearm?

There's a difference between America
And my America, you better wise up

I ain't got no crossover

The only Ivy League around here
Are those weeds growing around that mailbox

My back is a Picasso painting
You ain't brave enough to frame

Don't you feel sorry for me
I'm at home

Feel sorry for these lames
They say I'm

Lazy

Guess they don't know how hard it is
Making death look this easy

Banging their head against the bricks
Like I give a shit about they're 5 year plans

Like a rehab coffee shop ain't just good English for
Handout

Like a bookstore ain't a cancer ward
For us born losers

Shit
I'll pass on that

I gotta enough liquor right here
To make a Rhodes Scholar my brother

This is a charmed life

I draw buildings in the dirt
And call it Boardwalk

I can wrap my arms around everything
Worth dying for
Sometimes
They don't make it that far

But its all mine
Ours
Used to be yours

So why do you hate on my scars
Like you don't have a matching set?

Like you ain't never traveled down
These navy blue tracks

Why
Does a dog enjoy the scraps
The butcher tosses it?
Why
Does a battered woman
Think a man with a stomach
Full of needles
Has room left for her?

Because the ghetto loves me
I'm a lot of things man

Ungrateful ain't one of them

The ghetto loves me
Why wouldn't I
Love her back

21 Gun Salute for Jesse Jackson from Huey P Newton

I will not come to you in a dream
Nor nightmares chaperoned by crescent moons

No chimes
Or squeaky floorboards will trumpet my arrival

But I will be there

Corner pocket of the limo arriving at your home
Always the fourth caller on your radio show
I will be clean
Baby faced and Afro picked to perfection
In your front pew for your opening sermon
Don't expect me to call you Reverend, Jesse
We Marxist
Don't swell our bellies
With the enigmatic chants
Of organized religion

One wonders
How you have ample time to castrate black men?

To lap at the blood of martyrs you were never great
enough
To overshadow
Though never honest enough to admit that you couldn't
topple

How does one travel so well
Only armed with an agenda?

My rifle was always too heavy
To run in circles as you do
I've heard the cockatiels in Oakland
Wear armor made of Chicago pigeons
They are

Curious birds, Jesse
Too endangered to believe in
Wealth or racist apologies for a fee
Do you see the pigeon's eyes?

Large as sunsets

Like they can visualize an enormity
They can never realize
The way their head bobs back
And forth
In and out
Of sunlight and attention
Pecking at the crumbs dropped by greater beings

Does this bird strike you familiar Jesse?
Prancing in-place, in shit
Limited to brief flights of fancy

Second fiddles should be made
Of thicker stuff

I will not trade demons with you
Like you would not trade your profits
For the bullet in my left shoulder
My exile for your absolve
Of white public figures that need urban backing
Your rubber stamp with
$30,000 admission fees
And two drink minimums

What is the going rate on Negro decency Jesse?
Will it fill a project bathroom?
The expired shells of my shotgun?

Is it a mushroom cloud above your morning cereal
The vapors serenading your nostrils

Have your knees gave up on marching Jesse?

Have you started to flinch again, when passing barking
dogs?

How many deposits does it take
To curb one's fear of fire hoses?
Has the immunity to the Montgomery
sun washed over you?
Like spit over a colored boy's forehead
Like the wind sweeping the suspended toes
Of lynched freedom fighters

You stand erect and in good health
Never a threat of colonialist progression
A hound the FBI never bothered to collar
A rabbit that watched from thick brush
While hunters took aim at Lions

You were never big game Jesse
How brazen a shield Martin must have made for you
I was closer to the balcony of the Lorraine
Than you claimed to be

The dark secret tucked into the back pocket
Of a pointing silhouette

A whipping boy for Malcolm's Uncle Tom jabs
Does the swelling below your eye
Ever fester
Throb with lost relevance?

Grew your disdain for men who embraced the light
Strengthen your resolve for Martin's charisma
Harold Washington's history

Do you really think
You're the first nigga
To call Obama a nigga
Jesse

How will Homer sing of you Jesse?
Does a plebe stand to be worshiped
In a golden state that deemed me Jesus?

Do you still forgo speeches at the top
Of step ladders in Harlem?

Do you see my name woven
Into wicker chairs?

Is the spear too heavy Jesse?
Who will speak of your struggle?

The council you gave a president
Before fathering a child out of wedlock

The mole you became for Castro
In exchange for 21 hostages

Is the spear too heavy Jesse?
Will they mourn you?
Broadcast your Operation PUSH declarations
Your presidential race concession speech
Will they cover mirrors in Hymietown
At word of your passing?
Will we remember any other color but green
In the Rainbow Coalition?

What happens to a civil rights leader deferred?
Does it dry up
Like a heart in a marksman's sights?
Or fester like a sore--
And then run
For president
For currency
For relevance in a world

It creates its own demand for
        Or does it explode?

In the event you are caught behind enemy lines

...and then tortured

The first thing they teach you
Is to make the room yours
Even though it is your prison
Imagine
Your full length mirror
On the western wall
The escalating engagement photos
                    To your right
Your feet
Resting upon the rug
Your wife picked out two Easter's ago
The chair you are bound to
Is now the recliner you took
From your father's storage

In the demon hour
You are left to ponder your faults alone

            In lesson two
They tell you to concentrate on
Three memories
Make them specific and rotate them
With precision

            Your wife's eyes when you brought
                    The puppy home

            The first time you got the Chrysler
                    Up to 105 mph on the highway

            Seeing sold
                    Next to your canvas
                    at the open gallery
                    On your 24th birthday

During the interrogation
When they say your name
Curse your god
Burn your flag with their tongues
You are taught to bait
        And switch
Replace your name in your ears
With honeysuckle
Or velvet
Anything softer than the blow you know
Is coming
Try blue ribbon
Or moon dust
In case you can feel the blood running
        From your ears

When the crowbar ascends to heaven
And you wait for it to be cast out
Across your forehead
You are taught to do two things
        First
Roll your tongue back like cobras
At the sites of lovers
So you do not bite clean thru it
        Second
Accordion your stomach
Till the palms of your diaphragm
Meet
Internalize the pain
You can actually control
Try to break the balls of your feet
Against your wife's rug
If it helps you forget
The metallic blur
In your left eye

        Lastly
Do not let
Your cheeks reveal anything

Your throat has sworn an oath against
Hide your breaking points
Behind your prayers
Though you should smile at these
Terrorists
If it keeps you from passing out
      At the precipice of rescue
Remember that no one answers calls for help
Yell fire instead
Behind enemy lines
Await flash
      When you yell thunder

You have been trained in these techniques
With the hope
You never have to use them

When the first piece
      Of her luggage
            Deafens itself at the bottom of the stairs
You try make the room yours again
A full length mirror on the western wall
That hasn't been shattered yet
Escalating photos to the right
With a woman that doesn't
      Hate you
And a man you envy
More than sunshine itself
When she stares at you
Chained in silence
You rotate your futures
With precision

      She buys your latest failure
          Anonymously out of sympathy

      Drunk and speeding
          Too lucid to read the speedometer in your
          Chrysler

Praying for brick walls
And vacant school buses

A Rhodesian Ridgeback dog
      Growls at your approach
      And no longer remembers your scent

When she says your name to console you
Replace it with train tracks
Fiberglass
      A rusted-out trumpet
Spittle dying a slow death
On the mouthpiece
Name yourself diamond
Or rebar
Anything softer than the sound
Of the front door opening

When she goes to grab your hand
Ball your fist
Till your fingernails
Find oil in your palms
Hug   yourself   so   hard
Your ribs scream in dead tongues
Till you forget that she is
Making love to your forehead
With an ax

She will keep talking
But all you can answer back is
FIRE
     FIRE
         FIRE!
At the top of your lungs
Your home is a moth
That cries gasoline
You want to escape
But outside there is only
Thunder

For you
> Your flash
> Was never necessary

You laugh
When her eyes catch you
In the rear view mirror
It is all you can do
To keep
From collapsing in the driveway
A metallic regret
Fills your mouth
As she drives away
You realize
You forgot to protect your tongue
And you wonder
> If this
> > Is really
What you were trained for

Quartered

The third motor cries in its genesis
The ground is unflinching and rude
Against your spine
Wooden sacrifices and splinters
Rest below the small
Of your back
It is not until the fourth engine
         Coughs
That you remember the scorching
Around your ankles
The rope pythons
Strangling the bullet trains in your wrists

         Your fingers firework from your palms
The blood rushing from your knuckles
Like a waterfall unsure of its future
Tip-toeing along the knife edge of a cliff

The sun greets you as the earth
Retreats from your shoulders
You feel the elastic of your torso
Age and crack
The joints of your frame
         Slowly unhinge
Your ribcage bites down
On its screams

The moan of the jeeps
Vibrate your limbs
Like the wooden planks
Of train tracks

Your dismantling in four acts

As the wheels crawl
The distance between your sight
And praying pegs grow

Before your left shoulder
Finds liberation
Behind a four wheeled
       Tubman
You kiss the left seams of your chest
As you remember

That your mother gave you that

Farragut, TN (1:30 PM EST)

At 1:30 pm
The sun is highest in the sky
I am driving thru Farragut, Tennessee
    The last face of color I will see
Is in the reflection of a store front door
That is carelessly let go in my face at a gas station

    In Farragut
Holding open a door for me
Will get you called a nigger lover in the backroom
    A longer wait to be seated
    At the Cotton Club

Don't let know passing negroids
Disturb the stitching of your social fabric

The walls are sweating pig's blood
Behind the store fixtures
Gather steam in the throats of pundits
Resentment soaking the knees
Dipped in southern pulpits

    Tell me Farragut
Who do I have to ask
To ask for my forgiveness?
Lord knows we don't apologize for ourselves

Fill couplets with faith
And separate but equal mantras
Like heavy robes
On the neck of holy men
In valleys they don't believe in
There is a tempered steel
Under the tongues of these residents
    A rising bile
Grandmamma taught them
To sing from their diaphragm

I stare upwards into the blinding white
And see eagles circling

     In Farragut
Even the vultures are only born
With right wings
Speak with claws
Meant for my liver
As if I were Prometheus growling
     Fire to their
Brush covered serenity
I am a bloody nose and
Ligature marked wrists away
From fitting in
An Alaskan pants suit statue
Is erected in the cheeks of every bystander
I pass

     In Farragut
Obama is a virus you catch from being lazy
A neglect on voices
That died to keep the insulation thick
With flem and pick-up trucks
If the oval office is 513 miles from this intersection
Then Farragut's best and brightest
Are conceiving a slingshot
     That will project 514
They drink with gerbil cheeks from this fountain
So full
The cyanide actually quenches
Their thirst
Tingles between the toes
When wading in rivers
That will never flow upstream
Here

     In Farragut
They shake hands with their eyes
And none have privileged me

With the flags even half staffed
The sun is highest in the sky
And I am the iodine drop
In their whole milk
The Viacom hustle
In their moment of silence
For confederate generals
And America the way
        It was intended
        The way it was written
With crowbars and fire hoses
Into flesh

It is 1:30 pm
But only newspapers discarded
In waste bins will tell you the year
They grind past me
Evading the diluted space
That drips under my feet
Secretly hoping the closing door
Will mouse trap me
In its sliding track
Yet, here I am

        In Farragut
Paying for gas
A drink
To combat the glowing white of the sky
And safe passage
Back into the present

Dear Joseph

Dear Joseph
I would say that I am sorry
But I don't want my first words to you
To be a lie

I am sober
I am granite
I am completely alone
Except when I summon you
I do so now
Because your mother
Had poor eyesight
She could not see your future
Like I could

I say this letter aloud
As they do not let me handle pencils
Or scribes in here
I mark my days on the cell walls
With the blood of my knuckles
The bars are not quite the soft landing
Your mother's cheekbones
Used to be
But we all sacrifice a little
For something greater don't we
Like the way she sacrificed her forearms
For the beating her language
Should be taking
There were no raised voices
In my house Joseph
That weren't coupled with another legacy
Parked in her stomach

But she loved me
I was Granny Smith rotten some days
And she would endure
The tornado of my belt

Until my shoulders were exhausted
And needed to be taped together
By her embrace
I am not ungrateful Joseph

I am big picture smile
When I think about having a son
Your mother didn't understand that marriage
Means yes
And now
When a woman says I do
The word 'no'
Runs screaming from her vocabulary
She claimed I forced myself upon her
And contends this is a bad thing
Your sister is the gorgeous
Result of your mother's protest and wailing
How can this
Be called a bad thing?

She was lucky to have a man
That loved hard
Like a belt buckle
Like the whip of a metal clothes hanger
It just proves how much I cared
How else could I touch her
When I was given anvils attached
To my wrists
Bending your mother into a weapon
Suitable for me to yield

Joseph
Don't ever think I didn't love her
I just loved you more
And I know some pussified
Faggot that's never gripped a real woman will say

Yeah, you must have loved her to death, huh?

Your mother would spew buckshot
From her tongue
And I don't know any other way to grip a shotgun
Except to clutch the pump and squeeze thunder
From its barrel
Besides
If my mother
Was a beautifully broken mirror
That understood how to wear her bruises
Then why couldn't yours

We knew early
You would be a man
That you would have my snarl
My anvils
Your mother was convinced
That you could be anything in the world

Including your father

She had already made the appointment
At the clinic
Had already made arrangements
To be picked up afterward
And to be off of work
For a couple of days

I couldn't let her kill you Joseph

I couldn't bear the thought
Of you
On a table

Not

Whole

So I grabbed her
Around the shotgun

Until I could see the cherry blossoms
Bloom in her eyes
Until your heartbeat
Found a hiding spot
I would never
Go looking for

If you were going to die
You deserved a more honorable death
Then the hands of strangers
And sterilized instruments

Joseph

I am sober
I am granite
I am completely alone
Except of course
When I summon you

For the fledgling masochist – or 10 simple ways to get yourself kicked in the junk

One:
After you ask her about her day, wait thirty seconds before interrupting her by saying, "I'm sorry, I wasn't really paying attention." When she begins to repeat herself for the second time, get up abruptly and tell her your ex won't stop calling and is in a time of need. Please, don't bother to wait up and to wrap the chicken so it isn't too dry when you get home in case you have a big appetite at your return.

Two:
Only tell her you love her while she is in the act of going down on you.

Two(A):
For bonus aggravation, appear annoyed if she stops to say it back and claim she just destroyed your libido

Three:
When you attend her child's graduation, comment she looks *way* too young to have a teenage daughter. When she smiles at this, ask if her daughter dates older men.

Four:
If she ever complains about not climaxing during sex, tell her at least she doesn't have to think about her sister to cum like you do.

Five:
Tell her you like her so much better than your ex because now you don't have to worry about guys hitting on his woman in public.

Six:
Instead of apologizing for all the previous stated actions like you will never do anything like that again, stick to your guns and proclaim that you (as well as she) knew exactly

what you were doing, when you were doing it and don't plan on pretending you didn't just so she'll take you back for another month.

Seven:

Even after she confirms that you two are exclusive, show up at her lunch hour with flowers, Chinese food or promises. Ignore the absolute silence of her surprise or her cellphone vibrating constantly (she claims it isn't important enough to answer in your presence).

Eight:

When you think you're becoming too comfortable around her kids, do not stress when she starts becoming too busy to go out with you, but starts asking what nights you're available to babysit.

Nine:

Do not hesitate to say I love you back, even though she only says it to you after crying over the last stand-in that broke her heart. Your shoulder should always be the life raft for her to lay her head upon, even though she will never allow you to swim freely thru her rivers. Do not attempt ripples in the water.

Ten:

Try not to cringe when she meets you at the restaurant with another man and says this is the guy I was telling you about, he is so sweet and has eyes like the little brother I never had.

Eleven:

An extra bullet in the chamber. Be completely honest from the beginning, tell her you are looking for a long relationship and don't plan on looking any further after your first date. Don't try to hide your tears from her when gravity asks for sacrifice. Fold your heart small enough to fill the lines in her palms. Tell yourself, she didn't really mean it, when she said all the good men, were taken.

The Folly in Standing Up

Few things smell like Sunday
Like a boiling pot of red beans in the kitchen

Reginald knows this

The scent pulls his eyes open from his afternoon slumber
He has left the TV on
It buzzes like a sunrise
He is not ready to welcome
A high tide of History Channel

Destabilization for a veteran

At 68 years old
Reginald has forgotten about more things
To apologize for
Then times he deserved an apology himself
But the TV is asking 1967 questions
2K Reginald simply doesn't have answers for
Like why a North Korean sunset tastes metallic
How he could never wash the jungle
From between his toes

The remote control is buried in a tree stump
Three feet away from his rocking chair
But there is a folly in standing up
Like volunteering
Like letting your head be exposed
To the mercy of thick brush
A non-English speaking nightfall
That hates you
Hates you in Lao

Hates you
For fighting for a country that hates you

Traitor

Mutt

That dog don't hunt boy
Unless he buried everyone's shit first

Reginald can feel the snakes ascending his chair
The venom is mercy
Don't wanna bleed out in no rice patch
With some Huntsville peckerwood laughing over me
Best bite me now
Lest my squad call you a friend
Of the Negro

Keep your head low Re-Re
There's less armor on the back
Of this helmet
They'll make your dome blush
Like an ink blot
Tell command that the darkies
Got no sense of direction
Dead negroes can't pin no tales
On trigger happy donkeys

Keep your head low Re-Re
The ceiling fan ain't no rescue chopper
Don't know what's waiting for me
Back there anyway
Another dead minister
A Doberman extending from the ethos
Of a blue uniform
At least here I got a M16 chance
An AWOL shot at seeing 70
Ain't you heard the forest fire screams
The scratches the starving natives leave
On my chest trying to eat the ammunition clips
Across my belt
In the land of the Goukes
The porch monkey is king
Keep your rifle dry

And your eyes open when you sleep
Don't know when one of these good ol boys
Gonna be too high
To tell I ain't no 14 year old Vietcong
Too ashamed by the time they come down
They gotta hide me
In a murder hole
No thank you
Re-Re don't do haiku

Too many hung. Casualties. Looks just like Heaven's. One
hand clapping.

The TV is calling its documentary
A special
Like there's anything special about
The smell of charred meat
Where a village used to be
Re-Re wants to stand up
But he can't
Still trying to roll over
From that pretty girl before the others
Got their turn
Can't stand up mid stroke
Lest they believe
You're a faggot over here
Couldn't understand her
But tears are easy to translate
The numbness of a woman's befouled body
Only visits you in foxholes
Or letters to home
You sign as Thomas or Jonathan
In case the mail carrier grew up
With Trent Lott
Didn't have no Casius Clay celebrity
Couldn't Louisville loudmouth
My way out of coming here

Re-Re counts his days in racial slurs

And epitaphs
Just 284 *Nigger watch my back's*
Till he leaves the jungle
Funny how the concrete
Is softer than American irony
How the clouds will always look
Like a napalm sky

Few things smell like Sunday
Like the handle of a semi automatic
Messenger
But Reginald gets it
Gets his rocking chair
Will never be sacred ground
As long as he keeps a memory
He gets that apologies are lost in the winds
Of lands you never plan on returning to
Which is why
He will never ask for the ones

He actually deserves

Part B. The boat ride home is not nearly crowded enough.

Grown up Ladders

Bring the soil
Meet me in the backyard
I've got a name with your shovel on it
       Join me digging

I've been in the dirt before I knew you existed
My fingers claw until I reach silence
I threw my heart down in there
       And kept digging

I dig around it so I don't kill the compliments
You shrink wrapped it in
It drops a little further
Every time I clear more Venus from under it
       Pack the soil

Seal with your spit in case you leave me
In case you left your pelvis
On my coat rack
Your promises under my welcome mat
       Next to the pick axe I borrowed

There were Gibraltar's
In my past
I swung it like you kiss me
       With malice and closed eyes

No, you can't have my heart
It's all dirty and tired
And tired and yours twice over
       When it rains

There were roots in your soil
I was gentle in destroying them
Dressed them in handshakes
       Told them we would've been brothers

A next lifetime fraternity
I lie with my hands
	And fuck Gibraltar's with my eyes

Meet me in the backyard
I've got an oak tree
	with your spine on it

I dig behind your molars
Found the silence I was looking for
Found it dirty and slick
	From the hurricane

You keep in your throat

Feathers like Hammers (for Clyde Stubblefield)

Clyde only picked sticks when he was nervous
Clyde was only nervous around women
So working the stock room
In that Chattanooga boutique
Kept Clyde pickin'
Using ballpoint pens to give Mondays a little rhythm
He was supposed to be counting pantyhose with
They said, *make your mark with the black ink boy*
And get them pumps on the top shelf
Clyde grabbed that step stool
Called it throne
Took them size 12 pump boxes
Called them snares
Balanced clipboards on bookshelves
Called them symbols
This
Is how you stay alive in 1950s Tennessee
Hold sticks like feathers
But pound them like hammers
I said hold hammers
Between two fingers light as feathers
Like a wrecking ball wrapped in velvet
Like cuddling with a full grown lion
That's how you swing em
Try to take a man's mustache off with an ax
You hear that?

Ms. Sue from down the way heard it
Ol Melinda with the sleuth foot
Walked quick to get an earshot
Never heard angels horseplay before
Heaven don't usually knock before it enter
Best be ready
Heaven don't usually knock before it enter
But a drummer don't hear that
Just hear the base drum four seconds before its turn
Staccato taps won't get you in this door boy

Staccato taps won't get you in this door boy
Rat–tat-tat–Rat–tat-tat-Rat-tat-tat-tat-tat
Won't get you in this door boy
You better bang that wall
Bang that wall like Rome wants to greet you
Like a Clansman got a cross to bury
I dare you to ask

I dare you to ask that man about his shoes
I dare you to ask that man why his shoes so clean
I know he walked thru the mud just to get here
I dare you to ask Clyde why his shoes so clean
Left foot pounding that Floor Tom
Could make thunder in a turned over skillet
With that foot tap
Right foot like a Tell-Tell Heart on the floorboards
Keep the rhythm on earth in case *Superbad*
Didn't make it to Heaven
In case Hell still pulls a good crowd
This
Is how you stay alive in 1950s Tennessee

I heard a drummer once
Six years old and still flailing my arms
Like I knew Clyde was watching
I wanted to hear the bass drum
Knelt real close to know what soul felt like
That drummer let me do it
That drummer let me do it
That bastard let me do it knowing what would happen
I walked away bleeding from my right ear
And he said,
Take that with ya
Take that with ya youngblood
Now no one can ever lie to ya

My ear bled all night
I said my ear bled all night
And only stopped when momma played

Phyllis Hyman
Now I can't hear shit
Can't hear a damn thing out that ear
Except Satan laughing when it rains outside
Except that drummer smiling
When a hustler sweats
Clyde says that's truth being hard on me
Truth don't cure wickedness
Truth don't cure wickedness
It just makes the land too expensive
For wickedness to settle

That's what Clyde told me
Well, Clyde don't talk a whole lot
He let them sticks speak for him
Let them sticks stir fission in Atom Bombs
But Clyde
Don't talk a whole lot
Used to piss off Mrs. Baker that runs the market
Tired of watching Clyde pick them sticks
Mrs. Baker would tell him
Boy, you ain't got the sense God gave a mule
He said
Why would I?
I ain't know damn mule ma'am"

Clyde went right back to pickin
Wrist over wrist like he was trying to bang shackles
together
Wrist over wrist like he was trying to bang shackles
together
Wrist over wrist over wrist over wrist
Like he was trying to
break shackles

I heard a tale

I heard a tale tall as Goliath once
Young couple walked into the King Club

Before the band show up
Clyde slumped behind his tower
To let Hell sleep for another hour
Young pretty thing asked Clyde to play a bass line
While she sang
Asked Clyde to play a bass line while she sang
I wish she hadn't
Wish that silly bitch hadn't asked Clyde
To play a bass line
While she sang
Clyde let her off easy though
Let her off easy and didn't speak
Gripping his drum sticks hard because
They were trying to scream

Tell this heifer
We don't play bass lines
We play heartbeats
We play heartbeats
We play marches on the capital
We play waterlogged steps to the SuperDome
We play ?uestlove's train of thought
How dare you ask for a bass line while you sing
Some low-rent, sideways Aretha knock-off no less
Tell me this though
Tell me this though
Would you ask Jesus for Tap water?
Would you ask Houdini for parlor tricks?
Would you ask an Arch Angel to negotiate on your behalf?
No
No
You don't ask Monk to play the keys
You ask him to make a harp weep
You don't ask Jimi to play his guitar
You ask him to pluck a fault line
Till Jazz falls out

Be careful what you ask for
I say be careful what you ask for

I asked to hear the bass drum once
I still can't hear shit
Satan laughs in that right ear
Every time I say I miss my hearing
But Clyde ain't no monster
He let the sticks speak for him
Clyde ain't no monster
He just hides monsters in his drums
Hides them in his drums
Have you ever seen a man train monsters with
drumsticks?
Me neither
But I've never seen a man Jitterbug
During an earthquake either
But I believe it
Never seen
Clyde ask the clouds to put lightning in his hands
To birth thunder
But I believe it
I believe he beat that drum
Beat the drum like the monsters want out Clyde
Beat the drum like the monsters want out Clyde
Like the monsters want out Clyde
You hear that
James heard it
Charlie Patton can still hear it when he gets on his knees
You wouldn't know angels horse playing
If no one ever told you different
Wouldn't know a man was hiding a wrecking ball
Under a velvet cloak
Heaven don't usually knock before it enters
Heaven don't usually knock before it enters
Heaven don't usually knock, it just enters

Best be ready
Best be ready
Best be ready

La lluvia trae su nombre

By the time the first officer arrived
My right shoulder
Had settled under my chin
As if
        The joint was on a sliding track
        Connected to my sternum

My assailant lay dormant
A dent in his ribs
The size of ball/socket
        And gravity
Suppressed Spanish
Crawling under his labored breath
An iconoclast staring at the heaven
We fell from
The railing from the ledge
Still dripping the bravado
He boasted before
My cursive hand wrote
Onomatopoeia
Against the devil side
        Of his jaw

I could remember the peace-man's face
If my eyes
Weren't eight ball side pocketing
In my skull from the pain
His questions were booming
        And hollow
Like underwater gunshots
The tone changing
As he stared at the widest points
Of my body
Realizing it failed the symmetry
I had previously
Taken for granted

His sympathy came in the form
Of my shoulder
Coin slot
        Jackpotting
Back into its origin
The crash of a reloaded shotgun
Coursing thru my right side

To this day
I only remember the fall in tildes
A twenty foot drop
With another man's heartbeat
As my landing pad

I did not
Know
His girlfriend long

Possibly shorter
Than the Lucifer vertical
We both enjoyed
I'm guessing
She spoke native tongue
        To him
When explaining the fit of her waist
Against my forearm
The punctuality of my gaze
To her hips
As they dug into the matrix
Of the bowling alley
The arcade her accent
Could play on the same quarter all day

She would speak torpedo
Into my deepest waters
The Spanish words spackling
Between the existence of a boyfriend
She misplaced my knowledge for

I suppose that pollen doesn't always
Owe the wind an explanation
For carrying it away

My swift may have been overrated
Back then

Perhaps she is the reason
I cannot throw a fastball
Without her Saint Eurosia hair pendant
            Rotating in my throat
Her fingernails Golden Harp-ing my ribs
When I reach up to kitchen cabinets
Why I can never make it thru a
College Spanish course
Or feel the weight of her voice
On my collar when it rains

It is possible
She is more majestic in the ache of my shoulder
            Than she ever was in real life
That the throb in my collar bone
Has a native tongue
To rival her goodbye kiss
That she saw a skinny black teen
As more spaceship

Than anchor

Or oak tree

You Revolution, You

*'Sometimes people carry to such perfection the mask
they have assumed that in due course they actually
become the person they seem.' - W. Somerset
Maugham*

Look at you
You cute
     Revolution you
You came from nothing
Nothing but hand claps
And lepers
You breathe cinder
Bloody your hands
     Never
Snake bite your art
With replaceable fangs

You got rapture in your lungs
Castrated mountain summits in your throat
You tell magnificent fables
Hard-living by proxy
Sacrifice is beautiful
     Even if you don't own
     The black eyes
But you got fans now
You got a staircase in your sternum
That bypasses your heart
Thinned your skin for the occasion
Grew your hair out
Past your vision
Twirl it with your ring finger
Till it's caught in a class ring
You forgot all the patrons to

You
Beautiful
Revolution, You

You save lives
As long as the airfare is expensed
Shake hands with the sincerity
Of a two-story plunging
Manhole cover
Blow kisses thru
Gritted teeth
Licking the sunlight
From the enamel

You tell the horizons
The fault of its latitude
You broker inspiration
Believe cancer
Makes for a good story
Catch the 11 o'clock
To theme your next project
You birthed a daughter
Named her satellite
Fathered a son
And charged him a credit
To carry your junior
The moon sliver
Envies the inside of your ribcage

You've got more blood in your ears
Than plasma in your conviction

Your canvas has Berlin Borders
A following that mispronounces
Your government name
You love
Like cigarette ash
Burning the fore knuckles
Replace your contacts

With camera flashes
Release a sex tape
Of you
Masturbating in a dark room
      While sobbing
Pay a stranger to abuse you
Before you climax

Here is the here after
You've been lusting for

The reason you only answer
Family phone calls in a crowded room
Why you can't swallow food
Unless you close your eyes
      And imagine
They served your pride
At this diner
Wonder why the moons
Have forgotten your orbit?
Why Satellite has hated you
For years now
Juniors are too expensive to franchise
They will bludgeon you
With what used to be
You
What you were
Before you were you

You
Adorable
Revolution
You
Have a better story

Assuming
It's yours
To tell

Forest Fire

When I kiss you
Under this tipsy sky

Will you resurrect me
Before it wakes up?

Before the clouds get their bearings
And discover my body wrapped in silkweed

Traces of your voice
Still
Leave bruises
On my shoulders?

Can you steady your hand
When you break me?

Reshape me as a sun dial
I am always useless

When your light is taken from me

Like the Earth was allergic to my parallel
And refused to let me fall

The magnets in your cheeks
Is a smile I could never pull away from

Tell me where the sidewalk ends

Tell me this temple you've been building
With walls made of nothing
But the sound of you sleeping

I will rest there like a wounded soldier
His memory cut out during battle
Sleep under my shield

So I am not devoured by your reflection

I will draw the ocean
You dream of being rescued from

The scarf you think is too warm to wear
On most days

The wind at your back is a reminder:
Nothing can move you

Not a boulder ignorant of gravity
Not a blizzard who only wants to spin unto himself
Till he is spun back into his beginning as a snowflake

I miss you

I miss you in a way
A needle misses the inside of forearms

How guitar strings hate to love the notes
That leave it

I bring this forest fire to your open sky
Please see
That you are above majestic things
Destroying themselves

Lock your ankles to summits
And watch you move mountains
When you dance

This waltz of volcanoes imploding

You dip your toes into the pain buckets
And watercolor a God's face
Across this landscape

When I kiss you

Under this tipsy sky

Would you tell my mourners
I died a hero?

Hold me like a noose
When you hang me from your lips

I bleed sand between
Your hourglass fingertips
Dying

Always felt comfortable
In your hands

Every night
The sky drinks its own weight
In your eyes

It is too drunk by dawn
To fight off the coming day

We are all numbing the pain
Of losing what we never really deserved to have

Flying kites during thunderstorms
Trying to forget the taste of safety
On our tongues

When I kiss you
Do not be ashamed to carry me home

Though I'm sure
I've never been there before

Blacksmith

Along a cobblestone entry
Where the grass has grown
Between what is assumed
As stable footing
Fire and bending steel
Cocoon their way around
        .   A man at work
He is a diligent slave
A soul that has welcomed eternity
My heart is helium bursting
Hoping he still hears earthbound pleas

He is a blacksmith
        He is building my future son

The difference between entitlement
And greed
Is a talent wasted on humans
But how do you pray
With your arms folded?
Fingertips excavating your ribcage
For passed over promises
At the expense of a healthy child
I am not built for the fate
Of ten toes and deductive reasoning
The broken planet
Dangling on celestial wire
        Requires more these days
Painted faces pulling switchblades
From behind your ears
A hand grenade under a rainbow
Handkerchief
What magic tricks
Will breathe upon newborns
Young boys delivered into
Upended broken
Bear bottles

Blacksmith
I bullet express you
The anatomy of my son

Bind his spine in bamboo
To lash back at those that would lash his back
When crossing borders
Or jet stream conviction
Give him bookshelves for collar bones
Put the burden of knowledge
On his shoulders
The blood of Atlas
Thick enough to collar
Him
A neck of fused glass
That will break clean
Before rope burns occur
Aluminum shafts from the knee caps down
Saltwater in his lungs
That will boil from the tar pits in his throat
The words will flow pure
And lucid
Humble Shell Casings
Melted into sheets for his torso
An axis in his hips for perspective
Fingers made of cocoons
Beauty springing from everything he touches

Blacksmith
Give him his mother's eyes
So he'll never see the world dying
Before him
There is a conviction in your tools
A tolerant pleading in the sparks
Of your pounding steel
Place your native tongue in the hammer
The regrets of your makers
In his elbows
They should swing free

Like a Jesus lynching
A nose bleed in a hurricane
He is worth the bending
Worth your crafting
Of discarded planets
Seldom traveled sidewalks
Cups that overflow
But are never drank from

Build him true
Build in him your favor
He will be the first
            To thank you

Beautiful Biology (*after Ed Mabrey*)

Ever since 7th grade
I've dreamt about holding your hand
With my left hand
It still
has grip
left in it
I never forgot how you gave me that Valentine
In Mrs. Saunders home room
When nobody else even
Stopped at my desk

You always smiled at me

And if I died tomorrow
I'd want to be buried in your dimples
So I can be reborn
Every time you laugh

In music class
The whole room would laugh at me
Because
I couldn't really sing
But you said that was because
God put my singing voice
On the inside
And that my heart
Must sound like a soldier
Coming home from war
And seeing his daughter
For the first time

When Thomas pushed you down
At recess
I picked up a rock and threw it at him

With my left hand
It still

has grip
left in it

And when all his friends called me stupid
And retard
And dummy
You called me that night at home
And said thank you
I held the phone up to my ear for an hour
After you hung up
Because I was scared
If I did too
I wouldn't be able to feel your voice
In my head anymore

When we graduated
My stepfather told me to stop staring at you

That you were like the sun

And we shouldn't look too deeply
Into things we can never touch
But mom thinks nothing is wrong with me
She calls me
Beautiful biology

Its been 12 years
Since homeroom
I see you every day
When you get off the bus
And you still smile at me
Even though it hurts sometimes
From your busted lip or bruised cheeks
I guess Thomas
Still pushes you down

I'm sorry
Sorry I'm like this
But God made my arm bent

In an 'L'
So it was perfect for me
To walk you down the aisle
Or hold our child safe and secure
And my leg is twisted
So I can't dance
Around your feelings
Or kick you while you are down
My speech is slow
          And slurred
So I have time to think about
Everything that I say
And will never say something to you
That I don't mean
You've been my wife since 7th grade
But I've been waiting on the right time
To tell you

My heart sings your name
Through my veins
Falsetto's your shape thru
These twisted lips
And abstract limbs
I never hung up that phone
So I still feel your voice in my head

Now that is beautiful biology

That is a no brainer
Dumb or stupid
To think I'd give up on us
Makes me want to grab you
And kiss you like I am a soldier
Returning from war
Like you are a sun
Worth catching fire for
But only with my left hand
It still

Has grip

Left

In it

Until then
I'll be here
Waiting for you to get off
That bus
Saying anything to make you laugh
So I can be reborn again

At least for one more day

To Dine on Man

She flirts like a bullhorn. Smiles a meteor shower when
you ask her name.

       That is the first deception

It will be unpronounceable.   A metronome that breathes in
4x4 time, if you snap on beat, you'll find the matchstick on
her tongue will light for you. She'll speak comet and dare
you to kiss her. Lock her arms into crocheted songbirds
that are immune to stasis.

The blood in her giggle is a warning. If you've felt her
heavy on your hip bone, you've stayed too long.

The miss in her phone call is a lie. She knows your
addiction is more volcano cough than ash coating the
lungs. She can squeeze her thighs together and pull your
ear from down the hall like a dog whistle.

       Her whistle
               across your chest collapses the levees in
      your heart. Grounds the flight in your opera.

Her name? It has to be tip toed for her to recognize.
Hummed for her to respond in earnest. A blood canticle to
wrap her lips around.

If you're lucky, you can mimic the tap of her tongue against
your teeth.

If you're touched, it will happen

            In 4x4 time